NEPAL
The Himalayan Kingdom

NEPAL

* The Himalayan Kingdom *

Photographs:
MANI LAMA

Text:
ARATI THAPA

Lustre Press
Roli Books

ISBN: 81-7437-067-6

© **Lustre Press Pvt. Ltd., 1996**
M 75 Greater Kailash II Market
New Delhi 110 048, INDIA
Tel.: (011) 6442271, 6462782,
6460886-0887

Fax: (011) 6467185

Conceived and designed by
Pramod Kapoor
at Roli CAD Centre

Printed in Singapore

Contents

—— ✳ ——

Preceding pages 2-3: A jhankri *(shaman or a bonpo) standing on top of a mountain in Gosainkund.*

Pages 4-5: Akash Bhairav displayed during the seven day Indra Jatra festival honouring Indra, the king of gods.

Pages 6-7: The Sherpa people greeting the rimpoche (high Lama) of Tangboche monastery. The Sherpas are known worldwide for their mountaineering skills.

Pages 8-9: A panoramic view of the majestic Mount Everest from Gokyo.

Pages 10-11: Bhairav and Ganesh looking down at the Indra Jatra crowd from a window, while waiting to take their place with the Kumari, the living goddess in the festival procession.

12

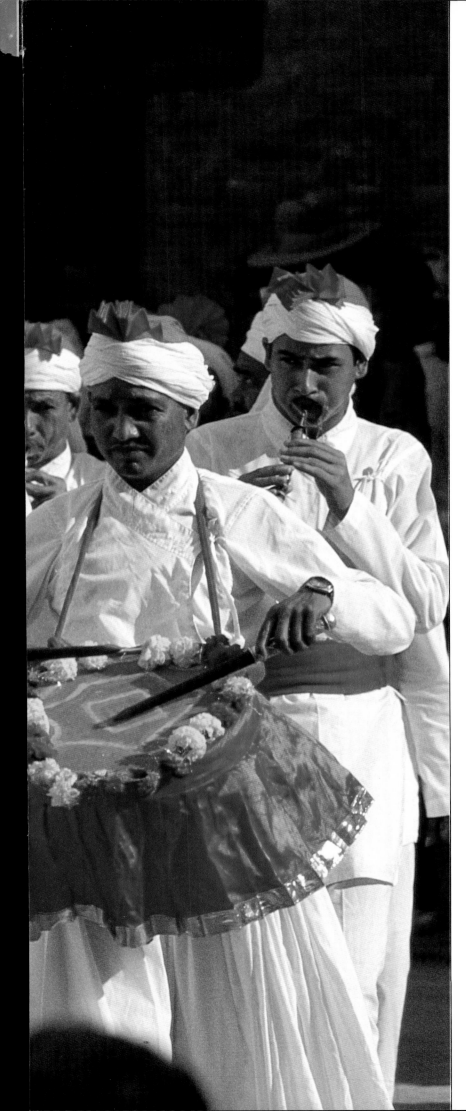

This page: An old Gorkha army band (musicians) on parade during a festival.
Following pages 14-15: "Never a wink". The eyes of Boudha and the pigeons.
Pages 16-17: Mataji meditates with lights in her puja room. Matajis have a divine power to heal possessed persons.
Pages 18-19: Village Phoolpari near Dhulikhel with the mustard in full bloom and the Himalayas in the background.
Pages 20-21: An aerial view of Boudhanath stupa. Many Tibetans have settled around this area. Boudhanath is known as an international Buddhist centre because all the different monasteries are located here.

13

Chapter 1

——— ✳ ———

Introduction

$\mathcal{O}$nce upon a time, or so goes the legend, there existed a valley amidst beautiful mountains. In this valley was a lake as blue as the sky. And in the centre of the lake rested a lotus that radiated magnificent and sparkling rays of the purest blue. The rays spread far and wide creating a celestial atmosphere so powerful that it drew divine attention. Legend has it that Manjushree who was passing by was so charmed by the beautiful sight that he caused the water to be drained with a swipe of his magical sword, so that a holy city could be built there and its people would live close to the gods. Thus was created Nepal—the abode of gods. The lotus, according to legend, was the manifestation of Lord Swayambhunath who stands tall today as the protecting deity overlooking the city and guarding it against all evil. The spectacular pair of divine eyes painted on the stupa ('chorten' in Tibetan) that surveys all of Nepal is revered by Tibetans and Nepalis alike who constitute the major population of the country.

Sifting facts from legend might not be easy in Nepal where the two are deeply entwined. Moreover, there are no sources of written documentation. But today, geologists claim that Kathmandu valley did lie under water at one time. Ask any Nepali and he will proudly tell you the story of how this magnificent country came about.

Legends are many, handed down from generation to generation, each surpassing the other in glory and fascination. In fact, it would not be wrong to say that no country in the world is perhaps so steeped in myths and legends as this country. In a country where literacy is at its lowest level, legends have become a way of life. Many of them are filtered while being verbally retold and passed on so that it is quite natural to encounter a variation of the same story. Nevertheless, they have become a part of popular folk culture, meticulously preserved from family to family.

Nepal covers an area of 145,391 square kilometers. Approximately 19 million people inhabit the land. It is a heavily mountainous country with about 14 to 15 percent land being cultivated. It has a multi-party parliamentary democracy headed by a figurehead monarch, King Birendra Bir Bikram Shah Deo. The Prime Minister of the country is Right Honourable Sher Bahadur Deuba, leader of the Nepali Congress Party. The official language is Nepali. There are more than 30 languages spoken and around dozens of dialects used in the hills by ethnic groups. Among these Newari, the language of the Newars is mainly spoken in the valley. Tibetan is spoken mainly in the hills while Indian languages mainly Bhojpuri, can be heard among the people of Terai or the tropical region of Nepal which is close to the Indian border. The Nepalese currency of about Rs 56.00 is equivalent to US $ 1.00.

The topography of Nepal can be divided distinctly into three main regions— the Himalayas or the alpine belt (highlands) mainly in the northern part of the

Facing page: Kala Bhairav at Hanuman Dhoka. Bhairav is the destructive form of Lord Shiva; therefore he bears a fearful look.

country. It is defined by its jagged mountain peaks and towering snow-capped range. In such wild terrain can be found the homes of Tibetans and Sherpas who live a hard life supported by the yak, a multi-purpose animal used for ploughing and carrying luggage. Its hair is spun into yarn and its meat is eaten with relish. Just below the Himalayas is the central belt or the midlands conspicuous for its valleys. This belt, characterised by adequate rainfall and a mild subtropical climate has been a favourite with the Tibeto-Mongoloid or the tribal group consisting of agricultural groups like the Rai, Limbu, Magar, Newar, Sunwar, Gurung and Tamang who have cultivated most of the land. The Kathmandu valley falls in this belt. Environmentally, it is proving to be a disaster and Nepalis are now moving on to the Terai or the lowlands which is the third belt of this country. The Terai is a flat, predominantly dry land, with sweltering summer heat. Enclosing this part of the land is the Siwalik mountain range. Nepalis here consist mainly of Brahmins and Chettris who have taken to paddy farming. Much of the rice or *'bhat'* which is so favoured by Nepalis is grown here. The Terai is generally known as the granary of Nepal.

In the early days the Terai was feared for alien diseases like malaria; in fact the disease was known as *'Terai lageko'* (infested with Terai, which was synonymous with the disease.) Nepalis who travelled to or returned from the Terai were usually made to gulp down a glass of water boiled with a twig of *'chirauto'*—a bitter herb known to ward off malaria. The ritual ceased only with the eradication of malaria three decades ago.

Prithvi Narayan Shah, the ruler of a small Gorkha province who later united all the small states of Nepal into one Gorkha kingdom described Nepal as a delicate root balanced between two big stones i.e., India and China. It is an apt description considering the fact that Nepal is a landlocked country flanked by India and China on both sides. Both these countries are known as the most densely populated countries of the world. Consequently, Nepal has had to tread very softly with regard to its diplomatic policies vis-a-vis its neighbours. Evidently, Nepal's interaction with these two countries have left remarkable imprints upon its history, religion and culture. Chinese goods are freely available and marketed here as are Indian goods. It is believed among the devout Nepalis that the Char Dham, the holy pilgrimage undertaken in the four directions of North, South, East and West must begin from the holy banks of Benaras in India. Millions of Nepalis live in India just as large numbers of Indian businessmen are faring successfully in Nepal. India provides much of the daily necessary needs of Nepal. By and large , all tourists travelling to Nepal must go through India. Marriages between the royal families of India and Nepal take place to this day.

A number of Indian Rajput princes and royalties took shelter in the hills of Nepal during Muslim invasions. One of them was Dravya Shah who captured Gorkha. Later it was from Gorkha that Prithvi Narayan Shah dethroned the Malla kings in Kathmandu in 1769 and laid the firm foundation of the first united kingdom. Nepal, plagued by internecine rivalry between the Malla rulers, underwent long years of political turmoil. The most famous of the Malla kings was Jayasthiti Malla. Generations later, the country was divided between Malla siblings. Kathmandu, Bhaktapur and Patan became examples of splendor and artistry as the rulers, the Malla brothers and sisters vied with each other in beautifying their kingdoms.

The aura of divinity which surrounds royalty persists to this day and till date the king is considered to be an incarnation of Lord Vishnu. Legend has it that one day a Jyapu (a farmer) was ploughing the field when he hit upon something hard on the earth. A closer look revealed that it was a broken toe of a statue from which blood was oozing out. As the earth was dug deep, out came a magnificent stone statue of Lord Vishnu resting on a bed of entangled snakes. He rests solemnly today floating on water at Budaneelkanth minus the toes accepting gracefully the prayers offered to him by hundreds of devotees except the king. A dream revealed to a king warned that a curse would befall him if he by any chance sought 'darshan' of this beautiful statue as he was an incarnation of the same god. Since then, no monarch has ever visited the place but instead offer their prayers to the replica of this very statue made especially for their worship.

Art and architecture in Nepal bears distinct features of Newari craftsmanship.

His Majesty the King Birendra Bir Bikram Shahadev and queen Aishwarya Rajya Lakshmi Shaha giving coins to the dancers at the festival.

Newars are recognised as master craftsmen of Nepal. During the Malla rule the Newars were able to give free rein to their imagination which they skilfully transferred to the various temples and 'bahals'. They were skilled in the art of metalwork especially copper, apart from wood work. Patan was the centre of Newari artistry. The city is still famous for masks and clay work which is made by the Newaris. The intricacy of woodwork can be seen on the struts that hold the tiered roofs of temples in Nepal. On these struts are sculpted the fine figures of gods and goddesses with their attendants dressed in fine, delicate jewelery. A fine example of this is the famous Pashupatinath temple that has doors facing the four directions plated with exquisite silver work. Only Hindus are allowed inside but the foreigners are allowed glimpses from the opposite side of the temple which stands on the banks of the Bagmati river. The holy river Bagmati flows through the temple, its still and deep waters waiting patiently to take into its fold the ashes of the dead. For on its ghats the dead are cremated and their ashes submerged as a stepping stone to the gateway of heaven. Even the kings and the queens are cremated here and here also live the aged and the sick for whom life has reached its end and death is only at an arm's length. Wrinkled, gnawed and suffering they wait day by day, night after night for the inevitable.

The long interaction of fact and fiction has given rise to another interesting belief in Nepal—the existence of a utopian Shangrila. Shangrila was a place where peace reigned and only the learned lived. Those who lived here were free from illness and the path to enlightenment was easy. Only the lucky few gained access here. In the years 1784-1942, Osma de Keros, a Belgian who delved deep into Buddhism came to a conclusion that a place named Shambala valley existed somewhere high in the mountains that fitted the description of a Shangrila. For Westerners the name Shangrila and the belief

View of Ganesh Himal and Swayambhunath from Kathmandu valley.

behind it is fascinating and appealing because of the beauty, mysticism and treasures—both material and mental—associated with it, almost like the El Dorado.

A Chinese surgeon Dr. Lao Tsin, in the 1920s, wrote an article about a valley in the mountains that enjoyed a relatively warmer climate and was inhabited by people who were scientifically advanced and could use highly developed mental telepathy. He had travelled these parts of the mountain with a Nepali yogi.

The belief of Shambhala is very prominent among Buddhists. It is supposed to be found far north of the Himalayas. Buddhist scriptures mention the existence of 'beyuls' or the hidden lands and valleys among the Himalayas. Many went in search of them in vain. The scriptures mention certain signs and indications that predict the right time to go in search of a 'beyul'. One of the beyuls mentioned in the scriptures is believed to be Khembalung, south of Makalu. Sherpas living here point out caves located here which have mystical and spiritual powers. Some Sherpas believed that Khumbu in Nepal was a beyul, therefore many settled here.

These beliefs combined with the lethal charm of fantastic mountainous scenery make Nepal a most desirable destination. For Buddhists all over the world, Nepal is a centre for pilgrimage as Buddha, prince Siddhartha Gautama was born in Lumbini in 543 BC which is located in southern Nepal. The first account of Lumbini was given by the Chinese Buddhist scholar Fa-Hien, who travelled to India in search of Buddhist scriptures. In 1895 archaeologists excavated the pillar that marked the Indian King Ashoka's first attempt at spreading Buddhism. It is a protected site and the Lumbini Development Trust is now looking after the building of a well equipped library here. A monastery is already being built as are gardens and hotels for the thousands of Hindu

Painting of Padma Sambewa.

and Buddhist pilgrims who frequent the site throughout the year.

Just as legends and facts are inseparable in Nepal, so is religion. Buddhism and Hinduism are so intertwined that it is difficult to separate each from the other. Both the religions have a base of 'tantra', that was an import from India, along with shades of the most ancient cult of animism. While 'tantra' all but remains on stone and sculpture in India, in Nepal it is still practised during several religious rites. Interestingly, while the King is a Hindu, his subjects consist of Buddhists and practitioners of one of the world's oldest religion, the Bon. The Nepalis are very religious. In almost all households, every morning the head of the family irrespective of the sex invokes the deity of the house

Following pages 28-29: *His Holiness ven. Tushi Rimpoche offering fire puja at the reinauguration of Tangboche monastery.*

with the strong smell of burning incense burning on a bed of charcoal in 'dhapaoro' (a clay lamp with a handle) which is accompanied by the ringing of a bell in the hand.

Auspicious occasions call for 'puja' generally held with astrological help and guidance of the 'bahun' or pundit. It is performed along with the melodious sound of the blowing of the conch or the 'sankh'. Occasions can range from a new born baby's naming ceremony to appeasing the Sani god who may be playing havoc with one's career or marriage. No decision is taken without the prior consultation of the pundit who has a very important role to play in a society dominated by Hindus. Even the suitable date for embarking on a journey is chosen by him. Thus, in a society where religion plays a vital role it is not surprising to find Nepalis with heads bowed in deep reverence to all passing gods and goddesses while on their way to work or the marketplace, or of encountering little school girls and women freshly bathed, with a steel

A Nepali fortune teller holds the attention of a very interested crowd.

plate in their hands full with flower petals, incense and vermilion powder, the standard worshipping items.

Culturally speaking, Nepal is an amalgam of various ethnic clans and groups. While the alpine heights of the Himalayas which surround the country majestically are spotted with Tibetans and the illustrious Sherpas, the midlands are home to Rais, Magars, Limbus, Sunwars, Tamangs and Gurungs. The tropical belt is mostly occupied by Brahmins and Chettris considered to be of the upper castes. The caste system which was straightened and organised mainly during the Rana regime is still prevalent throughout the country.

Nepal is the abode of gods. Here the deities mingle with mortals. The beautiful snow-capped Himalayas where the gods and goddesses are said to reside look down upon the valley. Every Nepali will offer his prayers to the deities at least once a day while facing them. They are the natural splendor that surround the country. They challenge and beckon the fittest, that is why every year there are thousands of foreigners and natives alike who trek these foothills of the great Himalayas, fearless of the valleys and deep gorges that dot the mountains and which hide the mystery of some of the bravest men who never came back from their pursuit of scaling the great heights of the Himalayas. Yet many of them even dared to reach the peak experiencing 'feelings' that were beyond description. It is rare to come across someone who has not heard of Tenzing Norgay or Edmund Hillary who set foot together on the Everest peak. All these make Nepal a trekker's paradise.

These peaks rise to a staggering height of more than 8000 meters (26,250 feet). The highest Himalayan peak is the Mount Everest, 8,848 meters (29,028 feet) and extremely sacred to the locals. It is known as the Sagarmatha in Nepali (Mother of Universe), while Tibetans refer to it as the Chomolungma or the Mother Goddess. The other high peaks are Kanchenjunga 8586 meters, (28,169 feet) Makalu, 8463 meters (27,766 feet), Annapurna I, 8091 meters, (26,545 feet) Cho Oyu 8,201 meters (26,906 feet) Lhotse, 8516 meters (27,940 feet), DhaulagiriI 8167 meters (26,795 feet) and Manaslu 8163 meters (26,781 feet).

Mataji at the Machendranath festival in Jwalakhel receiving offerings from devotees.

Trekkers can take their choice of walking the countryside, the high mountains or scaling the higher ones in expeditions conducted with special permission. The trekking industry is growing at a phenomenal rate, earning the country's exchequer large revenues. Sherpas, mountain climbers well known all over the world accompany the trekkers as guides, porters and cooks. Most of them are now trained in environmental protection and are extremely aware of the dangers of pollution in the mountains. Economically, Sherpas are doing better than the rest of the tribals who live high up in the mountains facing the hazards of the altitude.

The rich flora and fauna found in Nepal have served the people of Nepal in more ways than one. For centuries Nepalis have made good use of 'baans' or bamboo weaving it into many utility items, the most practical ones being the 'doko' and cradles for new born babies, as well as decorative items. Nepalis have also learned to dissect and learn the use of several plants with therapeutic values in the absence of modern medicine, while many more are relished and have become part of everyday food like the nettle or a particular type of seasonal fern. The forests are full with patches of blooming rhododendrons and orchids of more than 300 species of which some are very rare. The sal and the champ tree found here are used in a variety of ways. While the former provides fodder and its leaves are weaved into throwaway plates popular during marriages and auspicious occasions, the latter is used for making reasonably priced furniture.

Left to right—Top: *A young Newari woman, a devotee of the Hare Rama Hare Krishna sect; A magar on his way to the market; A young magar woman from west Nepal.* ***Middle:*** *A Chettri porter carries a doko (bamboo basket) near Namche Bazaar; A Limbu lady shows off her traditional jewelery; A young Thakuri girl from Simikot (far west Nepal) wearing a shell ornament.* ***Below:*** *A young Gurung woman from west Nepal; A thoughtful Rai man enjoys the passing winter sun; A Brahmin woman with 'tika' on her forehead during the festival of Dasain.*
Facing page: *A young Tamang girl with rice 'tika' on her forehead after a puja at a festival. Tamangs are one of the major ethnic groups who live in the midland region.*

A large variety of butterflies and moths make the forests their home while more than 800 species of birds fly over the mountains. Animals like rhinoceros, 'gaur' and tiger can be found in the tropical lowlands, while the yak is the all essential animal in the mountains. Other wild life include langur monkeys, the dwindling species of crocodiles and the wild goat. The Wild Life Reserves and National Park have been established in Nepal with the aim of protecting and guarding these species. Wild Life adventure is provided almost round the year for those who are specifically interested.

One of the most interesting tribes are the Tharus with their fascinating aspects of Terai lifestyle, scattered throughout the Kochilla in the Eastern Terai, some parts of Chitwan and Deokhuri valley and a few places along the Karnali. It has been traced back historically that during Moghul invasions in India some royal Rajput women fled to the mountains choosing the Terai region. Perhaps, this was because of the hot weather to which they were accustomed. This also explains the pivotal role played by women in the Tharu community where men are almost subservient to women. Any Tharu male wishing to marry from his tribe must serve his would be in-laws for a year or two before the consent is finally given. A Tharu male must also open his slippers before he goes into his woman's chamber although this custom is fast dwindling. The women are clad in colourful skirts as opposed to ankle-length sarees worn by Nepali women. They also like to adorn their blouses with silver coins and shells. A streak of their fondness for jewelery is evident from the way the bedeck themselves with silver jewelery on their ankles, necks and arms. It is said that a single piece of jewelery is so heavy at times that it even acts as a measure of weight in the absence of one. Interestingly, for some strange reasons associated with their immunity to malaria, Tharus, who claim to be descendants of Rajputs, remained isolated from the mainland Nepalis until the disease was brought under control in the 1960s. They are mainly farmers by profession whose lives too have been changing with the building of roads and the advent of modern gadgets though it is not so evident as in the case of the Sherpas.

Among the other ethnic mix of people living in the hills of Nepal such as the Tamangs, Magars, Gurungs, Sunwars, Rais and Limbus are the Gorkhas. They are not a single tribe or an ethnic group as they are mistakenly referred to en masse. The word Gorkha is essentially derived from Gorakhnath, an ascetic and a devotee of Shiva who lived in a cave in the small province of Gorkha from where Prithvi Narayan Shah ruled and later captured Kathmandu. Gorakhnath was initially the patron saint of the Gorkhas. Today the younger lot of the Gorkhas would find it difficult to connect themselves with this remote hermit. A temple dedicated to him which looks like a normal house in located in Kathmandu Tole. The pride, loyalty and bravery of the Gorkhas have become a saga of lore and reality which reached its peak during the Falklands war. Naturally the original Gorkha troops came from Gorkha. These legendary brave warriors serve in the British and the Indian armies and have done their country proud time and again.

Facing page: A group of young Tharu girls wearing colourful traditional skirts in Dhangadi (far south-west Nepal). Tharus live in the Terai belt and were at one time known to be immune to malaria.

Chapter 2

—— ✳ ——

A Historical Overview

$\mathcal{L}$ike any other country with a monarchial past, Nepal's history is full of royal bloodshed, feuding principalities, kingly idiosyncrasies and passionate romances. In the beginning small kingdoms were found mainly in the Kathmandu valley. The earlier rulers chronicled are the Gopalas, Kiratis and the Lichaavis. Then came the dynasty of the Thakuris (considered to be of Rajput origin) which was founded by Amsuvarman.

In geographic terms Nepal is much closer to India; therefore cultural and political links were inevitable, but it was mainly Amsuvarman's specific efforts that brought these two neighbours together. He worked hard to improve ties and even gave away his sister in marriage to an Indian noble family. The Thakuri dynasty also seems to have introduced the system of dual rule in the kingdom. The dynasty's end came after Someshvaradeva (1178-1182 A.D.)

It was followed immediately by the Mallas, founded by Brahmadeva, a descendent but not of the same tree of the Thakuris. He defeated the kings of Kantipur and Lalitpur. During the reign of the Mallas, the kingdom began to forge a coherent identity regarding art, culture and politics which reached a peak during the final reign of Yaksha Malla who ruled for fifty-three years. But the Malla dynasty was marred by internal feuds among the power hungry nobility.

The most famous of the Malla kings was Jayasthiti Malla. Under his watchful eye the kingdom began to take shape in beauty and prosperity, for Mallas always returned with gold and jewels after their conquests which were used lavishly for the kingdom's artistic beauty. Jayasthiti Malla designed the splendors of his kingdom and the Newari craftsmen executed his ideas, their deft and agile fingers leaving a priceless heritage in wood, brass and copper that few countries in the world could match. The Newaris put their heart and soul into their creations.

Jayasthiti Malla's successor, Yaksha Malla worked hard to carry the legacy of his predecessor taking the kingdom's aesthetic glory to a zenith. His reign was powerful and peaceful but the legacy he left behind for his offsprings proved to be very different. Infighting and feuding politically drained the kingdom. Meanwhile other royalties taking note of the existing situation were attempting to make a bid for the kingdom. Finally when Yaksha Malla willed the cities of Kathmandu, Bhaktapur and Patan to his children, the disintegration of the kingdom was complete. Henceforth, the history of the reign of the Mallas was written separately in terms of these divided kingdoms.

Elsewhere in the valley, an ambitious but little known king was already planning the redefining of the Malla kingdom. This little known man was the ruler of the expanding Gorkha kingdom-Prithvi Narayan Shah-who pulled the

Facing page: *A festival crowd in Bhaktapur. The statue is the guardian deity of the temple.*

country into a modern era of history and went on to become the most well-known king. He also laid the firm foundation of a united kingdom.

A number of Rajput princes and royalties from northern India with their soldiers took shelter in the hills of Nepal during the invasions of the Muslims. Among them was Druvya Shah who along with his supporter was able to capture the hills of Gorkha. Prithvi Narayan Shah was the son of Marbhupal Shah, of the Gorkha kingdom. It was from the hills of Gorkha that Prithvi Narayan Shah pledged the unity of the Nepali kingdom and proceeded on a rapid rampage of conquests until he captured Kathmandu in 1769 AD with his trusted Gorkha troops, thereby avenging the humiliation of his father's unsuccessful attempt at capturing Kathmandu, and moved his capital to the centre of the valley. It is said that Prithvi Narayan Shah could accomplish this feat as he had marched into Kathmandu on the day of Indra Jatra when most of its people were drunk. He was a master of diplomacy, inspiring awe and

An old army on a parade from Gorkha. Gorkha was the province from where Prithvi Narayan Shah conquered and united the whole of Nepal under his kingship.

loyalty among his supporters for his administrative skill and craftiness.

After Prithvi Narayan Shah, his grandson Rana Bahadur Shah, still an infant, ascended the throne. The kingly affairs were looked after by his uncle Bahadur Shah. Having tasted victory the Shahs were not prepared to lie low. Under Bahadur Shah, the conquests for expansion continued, until the Gorkha kingdom covered the Himalayas from Sikkim to Kashmir. The awesome conquering spree came to a halt only when he met his match in the Chinese who repeatedly thwarted his attempts to invade Tibet. In fact, the Chinese later declared war on the kingdom, which they won, extracting a promise of obtaining recurring gifts for their emperor every five years. For decades the Nepalis undertook the journey through arduous, wild mountain tracks to present the gifts to the Chinese emperor. The practice came to an end only with the end of the imperial dynasty in China.

After this debacle, the Gorkhas, still undaunted in their quest for territorial expansion, turned their attention to the Indian side of their border where the British were by now firmly saddled. The British East India Company did not take Bahadur Shah's indomitable spirit of conquest lying low. Finally, Shah lost to the British General Ochterlony after their several attempts to invade India. Then came the Treaty of Segauli in 1816 that set the present boundaries of Nepal. The king had to give up a large part of the Terai territory adjacent to the Indian borders, and also had to concede to the British demand of posting their resident in the hitherto reclusive hills of Nepal. These British residents later assumed the role of ambassadors.

During the war with the British, one man-Bhimsen Thapa—had established his credentials as a brilliant statesman. He dominated the kingdom as prime minister for thirty years, and left his indelible imprint on its history. Unfortunately, he became a victim of palace intrigues. He was accused by the influential Pandes in the kingdom of murdering the son of a senior Pande queen and thrown into a dungeon where he committed suicide later.

In the same year, another infant—Rajendra Bikram Shah—came to the throne while palace administration was handled by the second queen and his step-mother. When the elder queen died, the junior queen restored the Thapas to favour. Some years later, the queen's trusted friend and alleged paramour Gagan Singh was murdered, presumably at the behest of Rajendra Bikram Shah. An enraged queen, fuming with anger and hungry for revenge, sought the help of Jung Bahadur Rana, a commander of the Nepal regiment, and ordered the nobility to assemble at the Kot (palace assembly). The commander let loose his men and the bloodiest battle in the history of Nepal ensued here, when the king was accused of instigating the murder of Gagan Singh. It is referred to as the 'Kot Massacre' which turned the tables in favour of the Ranas. Most of the nobility opposed to Jung Bahadur Rana were killed and he became the real power. Although the Shah king was spared, he henceforth assumed a titular role only. Gradually, royalty was relegated to the stature of obscure divinity. The Ranas ruled the country with iron hands for nearly a hundred years, dispensing justice with an autocratic roughness.

Meanwhile, in the neighbourhood the subjugation of India by the British forced Jung Bahadur Rana to prop up a strategy that would protect their independence. The British were eyeing the mountains and the presence of their residents in the hills was a perceived threat. The Rana reached a compromise with the British. The British agreed to look after the interest of the Ranas both internally (which included thwarting any threat from the Shahs) as well as externally (warding off hostile forces). The Rana returned the gesture by agreeing to send his Gorkhas soldiers as recruits in the British Indian army. Earlier, the British had been highly impressed with the Gorkhas during the border war.

Cosily settled in his Himalayan nest and protected by the British the Rana, unhindered and unopposed, gave himself the title of 'maharaja' making it hereditary. Thus while neighbouring India surrendered to the brutal colonisation of the British, the Ranas enjoyed their rule indulging in the best

Following pages 40-41: A Buddhist funeral procession in silhouette. They cremate the body and the ashes are washed away in the river.

that life had to offer. Their women followed the European fashion of wearing dresses with meters of clothes while the men built huge palaces in the true European style.

In 1951 King Tribhuvan Shah (given the title while still an infant) fled to Delhi in 1911. His contact with the world outside Nepal, exposure to progressive ideas and links with Indian leaders gradually brought about a change in the monarchial foresight. Meanwhile, India had gained her independence. The Ranas had lost their strongest foothold when the British gave up their hold on India. Simultaneously, their hold too began to loosen over the country they had ruled for years. Tribhuvan Shah returned to his country and dramatically restored the Shah rule by masterminding a revolution which resulted in the overthrow of the Ranas. A Tripartite Agreement between the Shahs, Ranas and Nepali Congress (People's Representatives) in the presence of Jawahar Lal Nehru of India set the eclipse on the Rana rule.

Kathmandu Durbar Square (Hanuman Dhoka) in the early morning.

Mohan Samsher, the last of the Ranas, had to abdicate power. Following this, a constitutional demaocracy was established in the country, setting the stage for a decade of the parliamentary form of governance, which in turn introduced the country to other advanced parts of the world. New vistas opened up with the flow of foreign aid and the first signs of a potential tourist industry were evident as mountaineers and trekkers gradually began to troop in.

In May 1956, the world saw the coronation of King Mahendra which royals and dignitaries from all over the world attended, indicating that this Himalayan valley was no longer reclusive. Following his father King Tribhuvan's death in 1955, King Mahendra was left with the enormous task of guiding his country through the most transitional phase and also preparing his people for general elections. This election in 1995 heralded the advent of the Prime Minister B.P.

Koirala of the Nepali Congress Party in the politics of Nepal. Koirala called for better developments with the country's neighbours, especially India which was the hot-bed of the Nepali Congress. The Benaras Hindu University in India where most of its leaders studied was the focal point of most progressive political ideas.

King Mahendra also introduced the Panchayat system that could enable a locally elected person to improve decisions taken by the Council of Ministers appointed by the king. King Mahendra died in 1972 and his son King Birendra Bir Bikram Shah Deo, the present reigning monarch took over. Educated in the West with considerable liberal views he amended the Constitution and gave the country the single party system. Today Nepal is the only country with a Hindu monarch. The country witnessed a series of changes in recent years—the most important being the Communist Government that came to power for a short time in 1995.

The small but strong army that Prithvi Narayan Shah of Gorkha commanded mainly comprised of Thakuri, Gurung and Magar men. They came to be known as Gorkhas-a name directly derived from the place they came from and Gorakhnath-their patron saint. In time there was a lot of intermingling among the people of Nepal and the Gorkhas. A Gorkha is often mistakenly referred to as the caste of an ethnic group residing in the hills. Yet, a Gorkha can be a Magar, Gurung, Sunwar, Rai, Limbu, Chettri or a Tamang. They are spread in the midhills of Nepal and have mainly taken to farming. In the villages a Gorkha soldier is highly respected. Some houses have families with generations serving as soldiers in the army. They are sturdy people with a commendable ability to adapt to the hardships of the hills and as they have shown in the latter years, of the plains too.

Any history of Nepal is incomplete without a reference to the Gorkhas. These strong men wielding naked 'khukuris' surcharged the battlefield in 1769 with their war cry of 'Ayo Gorkhali'. The Britishers were so impressed with their bravery and valour during the Anglo-Nepal war that they welcomed their service by recruiting them in their own army-an arrangement made with Jung Bahadur Rana. Their cheerfulness and friendly gestures won the hearts of the British and their loyalty towards the British knew no bounds. Recipients of the Victoria Cross, their role was almost always decisive in all the wars they fought, which took them to new destinations and far-off places like Persia, Mesopotamia, Palestine and Argentina. The British Gorkha soldiers are stationed in Hong Kong. But now, as Hong Kong gets ready to be absorbed into China, these brave warriors await the outcome of this tryst with their destiny.

Chapter 3
———— * ————
Art and Culture

$\mathcal{N}$epal witnessed an era of impressive architectural glory during the reign of the Mallas. The Mallas were in power from 1200 to 1769 A.D., the greatest of them being Jayasthiti Malla.

During the Malla rule the Newaris, popular today for their business acumen among Nepalis were blessed with a natural flair for art, wood carvings and paintings. They constitute the majority of the population even today, their sharp mercantile brains equalled only by their own thirst for art and culture. Most of the mask painters in Kathmandu are Newaris who do brisk business by selling them. Their artistry left its mark everywhere in Nepal, in temples, palaces, houses and markets. Single-handedly, the Newaris gave shape to planks of wood found in abundance in Nepal, turning them into intricately carved windows and doors, making courtyards and adorning them with brass, copper and similar other metals. Such fine work transformed Kathmandu into a rich and fine repertoire of art. The oldest of the pagoda style temples is the Changu Narayan. It is 12 km east of Kathmandu. It is a two-tier temple with intricately carved doors and window frames. All around the temple are priceless pieces of stone art in the form of mythical animals and images of gods and goddesses. The temple is dedicated to Vishnu. The struts that support the roof bear figures of religious deities and different forms of Vishnu carved delicately. Like all other temples and pagodas in Nepal, it is flooded with prayer flags. Built in 232 AD it is in the middle of a spacious courtyard. It stands today as a glowing tribute to the craftsmanship of the Newaris.

So skillful were the Newaris in their craft that it is said that a Chinese ruler invited one of them named Aniko to China. Here Aniko made wood and metal (namely brass and copper) sculptures and won the heart of the king. So popular did his work become that it formed the base of what later became the present day shape of the pagoda in China and Tibet, for he had taken with him the art of making temples with roofs that slanted from the sides. His work is still said to be existing in China.

The earliest efforts to enhance the natural beauty of Nepal was perhaps during the rule of the Kiratis when King Ashoka of India visited Nepal in an effort to popularise Buddhism. He raised a pillar in Lumbini marking the birthplace of Buddha. But these were more in the way of historical monuments and columns raised with the inscriptions of Buddhist teachings. The city of Patan is said to be founded by Ashoka who gave away his daughter Charumati in marriage to the local ruler Devapala. Here she founded the cities of Chabahil and Deopatan in the Kathmandu valley. In the city of Patan the four Ashoka stupas still stand historically marking the boundaries of this beautiful city. Patan was known and is still sometimes called Lalitpur or 'the beautiful city'.

Facing page: A procession of jhankris (shamans) heading for the Gosainkund festival which lies to the north of Kathmandu valley.
Following pages 46-47: Bhaktapur women and children during a festival, offering water to the thirsty festival goers.

It was Jayasthiti Malla who formally put Nepal on the Asian map as a country of art and prosperity. None of his descendents could match the fame and popularity he enjoyed. Soon the Malla magic began to dim until the four kingdoms, Kathmandu, Bhaktapur, Banepa and Patan were divided and given to the three Malla brothers and sisters, who tried their utmost to glorify their respective kingdoms. These four ancient cities stand proudly today displaying the splendor and beauty of the years gone by.

Among these Patan is essentially a Buddhist Newari city. The waters of the Bagmati river flow through it. It is the centre of Newari Buddhist religion and traditional arts and crafts. Yet there were also Hindu temples around the palace courtyard because of the Hindu rulers. The most famous part of this city is the Patan Durbar square leading to the royal palace complex. The palace houses three main chowks or courtyards namely the Sundari Chowk, the royal bath called Tusha Hitti and the Mool Chowk. The chowks are splendid examples of

Patan Durbar square. Patan is known for its metalwork, statues and other crafts.

Newari architecture. The royal bath or the Tusha Hitti is the most ornate and intricately carved bath place. Here the King Siddhi Narshin Malla stood or sat under the continuous flow of water from the conch shaped tap and rested afterwards, opening his eyes to the holy presence of gods and goddesses adorning the walls in stone.

In the southern Patan is the home of 'Rato' or the red Machendranath—the popular tantric god Avalokiteshwara. For the Hindus he is one form of Shiva. He is the guardian god of rain. According to legend it so happened that one day a king requested Machendranath to persuade Gorakhnath, the patron saint of the Gorkhas to release nine nagas—the rain giving deities. The saint had held the rain gods and only his guru Machendranath could order him to release them. Ever since then the festival of Rato Machendranath, a god in red and slanting eyes, is taken out in procession every year in a chariot for one full month and the appeal for rain is repeated by the people of Nepal. During the procession of Rato Machendranath nothing must come across the way. The festival is followed immediately by the rainy season. For Buddhists he is Avalokiteshwara, the compassionate Buddha or the rain god. In Patan he is the Rato Machendranath, while in Kathmandu he is the Seto Machendranath.

The five-storeyed Nyatapola Temple in Bhaktapur is the tallest pagoda style temple in Nepal with a height of almost 98 feet. It was built by Raja Bhupatindra Malla in 1708 A.D for the tantric goddess Siddhi Lakshmi. The stone steps leading to the sanctum sanctorum are guarded by pairs of lions wearing belts around their necks. They stand on each level of the plinth and are supposed to be ten times as powerful as the pair immediately below them. There are exactly 108, a number which is used in most Hindu religious rites. Wooden struts that surround this five-tiered temple depict the human form of the goddess. The huge steps have become a popular platform for people to

The famous hitti (water fountain) of Patan with beautiful stonework on the walls and a conch shaped tap. In the olden days it was used as the royal bath.

gossip, talk politics and generally watch the flow of tourists.

According to a legend, King Bhupatindra Malla had built this shrine for Bhairava. But as is recounted and told by all Nepalis, Bhairava can be a nuisance if not appeased in the way he may desire to be. Alas, in this case the king must have lacked in his offering somewhere for Bhairava started throwing his tantrums upsetting the king to no end. The priests were ordered to find out the reason for the God's anger whereupon they advised the king to install the goddess Siddhi Lakshmi at the stroke of midnight. Since then of course, Bhairava has been quiet.

The most important stupa of Nepal is the stupa of Swayambhunath on which are painted the omnipresent eyes of Buddha that sweep over all beings as if to warn the earthly creatures to do only the right things. The brightly painted eyes and nose that look like a question mark survey the valley with piercing eyes.

The round dome which stands elevated is the representation of all four elements, the fire, the earth, the wind, and the water. The steps leading to it are the symbolic steps to Nirvana. From afar the stupa gives the impression of the god wearing a tall golden crown, a round pointed umbrella providing the finishing touch. This is the oldest stupa, as old as 2,500 years old. It was here that Manjushree stood and emptied the water from the lake creating the magnificent place called Nepal. On any given day numerous multi-coloured flags inscribed with prayers and tied to strings dance gently to the tune of the wind. These prayers are said to be carried to the gods by the wind. Around the dome are the various forms of gods and goddesses in bronze, copper and brass metal along with small stupas and temples.

Swayambhunath is sacred to both the Hindus as well as the Buddhists. It is common to see Buddhists here with prayer wheels in their hands chanting *Om Mani Padme*, while Hindus may prostrate on the ground and apply the red

Swayambhunath Stupa. It lies on the top of a hill to the west of the Kathmandu valley. It is revered by Nepalis, Tibetans and Buddhists.

coloured 'tika' on their foreheads, folding hands in deep reverence, sending silent prayers to the gods while making rounds of the stupa.

The Boudhanath stupa situated to the east of Kathmandu is another significant work of art and beauty. Built on flat land it is surrounded by prayer wheels like the Swayambhunath stupa, which also has the powerful penetrating eyes painted on all four sides. It is here that a large number of Buddhists reside, tuning and turning their prayer beads and wheels. Under the inspiration of their religious and political leader, the reverend Dalai Lama, here they pray everyday for the independence of Tibet, while also celebrating the arrival of every new year or Loshar with passion and fervour .

Facing page: The watchful eyes of the Buddha at sunset. The eyes are almost omnipresent, protecting the people from evil.
Facing pages 52-53: Boudhanath Stupa with a full rainbow after a storm.

54

The Hindus flock to Pashupatinath mandir situated on the Bagmati river. The enormous display of religiosity reaches its peak during Shivratri, for Pashupatinath is a manifestation of Shiva. On this day devotees travelling from all parts of the country come to the temple carrying offerings of milk, fruit, sweets and flowers. It is one of the great festivals of Nepal. Pashupatinath or the lord of animals and beasts or Shiva or Mahadeva is represented by the 'lingam' with the head of Shiva carved on all four sides facing the four doors which is carved in thick sculpted layers of silver. He is worshipped religiously by men and women alike. Non-Hindus are not allowed beyond the gate. The view to the actual *sanctum sanctorum* is almost deliberately prevented by the huge brass *'nandi gaî'*, the mythical cow of Hindu religion. Facing south is the rear portion of the temple. There are steps leading to the Bagmati river and on the left side of this river stands the handsome sculpted idol, Quali with ringlets of curly hair and half his body immersed deep into the earth. It is believed that Quali is the god of *Kalyug*. Regular devotees claim that there was a time when only his head was visible. Today the sand has slipped off the idol showing the torso. It is widely believed that the day the whole idol emerges from the sand will be the doomsday of the earth.

This two-tiered temple is rich with wooden carvings of couples in playful moods, gods and goddesses. The four main struts, on the sides of the temple supporting the tiered roof bear the carvings of a ferocious looking animal. Its face and body resemble that of a lion, the front two paws displaying a clawing gesture, while it exposes a jutting human male organ clutched playfully by monkeys.

As elsewhere over the world the centre of sculptural art in Nepal is the

human form, both male and female, in the form of gods and goddesses accompanied by attendants. The female form is slender with an almost heart-shaped face and protruding round hard breasts, while the male form is more fleshy. Both the forms are bedecked with jewelery.

Some of the pillars which have inscriptions in the form of motifs and symbols have an originality of their own although some scholars maintain that there is a certain similarity with the Maurya art of India. Many of the scrolls and paintings have a character which is basically religious like the punishment in hell, offering prayers, gods and goddesses, mythical creatures and serpents, with a base of 'tantra' which also found its way from India.

Among the predominant races in Nepal are the Aryans and the Tibeto-Mongoloid race. While the inhabitants of the midhills are mostly Chettris and Brahmins, the hills are dominated by Tibetans. The majority of the Tibeto-Burmese communities such as the Rais, Limbus, Tamangs, Magars, Gurungs and

Dancing and celebrating the Teej festival. Women dress in red for this festival and pray for the long lives of their husbands.

Sherpas are scattered in and around the mountains. Majority of the Gorkha soldiers now so popular as a martial race come from these clans. Basically stocky and hardworking, these people have learned to work and live alongside the arduous hills. The main language spoken throughout Nepal is Nepali, the national language, although amongst themselves, a clan or a tribe may speak their own dialect. The Nepali script is the Devanagari script which is largely derived from Sanskrit, the ancient language of the learned.

The caste system is still very rigid in Nepal, first introduced during the Lichavi reign, then reorganised by King Jayasthiti Malla into four different categories namely, the Brahmins, Kshatriyas, Vaishyas and Shudras. Most of the high castes are farmers preferring the midlands initially, but now shifting to the low or the tropical lands. However, the Brahmins because of their priestly tradition which required learning, gradually entered the elite government services and also reached top bureaucratic levels. The sub-castes were a result of occupational categories; for example, tailors, goldsmiths, fishermen or cobblers fell into the lowest castes. Any house which bore their footsteps had to be thoroughly cleansed and purified preferably with the *Ganga jal* or *Soon pani* (water in which a piece of gold has been immersed) and cowdung. Nepalis also very religiously follow certain rites called 'samskaras', the most important of these being the Jatakarna (the birth ceremony). When a child is born in a house, the house is considered to be polluted until the ceremony of Jatakarna or 'nauran' (naming) is performed on the eleventh day. It is followed by *Annaprasanna* or the *bhat khuai*, when the child is at an age normally between six to eight months. From this period the child is weaned off from the mother's milk and made to eat rice, dal and vegetables.

During the ceremony close friends and relatives are invited to participate in the feast cooked for that day. Every guest playfully puts a finger laced with food inside the child's mouth enticing the child to lick it. Then comes the age of *Chudakarna* or *Chevar* (when the head of the male baby is shaved) followed by the threading ceremony. Among the higher castes it is also a ceremony when the boy is given the sacred thread or the *janai*, which is a vow to celibacy and a stern reminder that forbids him from committing sins. It is to remind him that he belongs to the highest of castes, the Brahmins and that he should uphold all traditions and customs adhered to by them.

A sadhu playing his flute on Shivratri festival. Ascetics gather during this festival at Pashupatinath from all over Nepal and India.

Gradually, it is time for the joyous rites of marriage and then finally on to the last stage of one's life-the Anthesthikriya or the death rites. The mourning period is for 13 days. The main mourners are the sons, who lead an austere life during this period eating a simple meal without salt, just once a day and sleeping on the floor. The rest of the family also avoids taking salt. The hard life the son undertakes during this period is in order to repay the debts to the mother. It ends with the ceremony of Godan or giving the cow to the pundit in the name of the dead. This ritual is believed to help the dead soul cross the deep and deadly river, the Vaitami, on the way to heaven. With the price of the real cow going up these days it can be symbolically represented with coins. Among the Newaris, an important custom is to marry off the girl-child at a tender age to the god Narayan represented by the bel (Aegle marmelos) fruit. This enables her to remain married even after the death of her human husband. Socially it allows her to be free of the stigma of a widow and enjoy divorce or remarriage because she is still married to the fruit. This is called the *Yihi* ceremony which is undertaken with the gaiety of a real marriage followed by a big feast.

An old Newari person undergoes the interesting ceremony of the Newaris known as the *Janko*, a sacrament which is undertaken at the age of 77,84 and 91. After the *Janko*, the old person (man or woman) is considered to have acquired the halo of divinity and on his death he will be eligible to be carried on a chariot. Each *Janko* ceremony takes him closer to the steps of heaven.

Young Nepali girls wear simple frocks and their transition to puberty, symbolised by the wearing of *guniu or fariya* (knee-length saree) is a ceremonial occasion. The young girl sits cross-legged on a mat while her parents put 'tika' on her forehead and present her with a *guniu or fariya* and the *chowbandi choli* (because it has strings on four sides) and a few pieces of jewelery. Henceforth, she will be usually dressed in a *guniu* or saree. On this occassion she is blessed by some close relatives and sternly reminded of her responsibilities as a woman. The men wear a long shirt known as *the daura*, and *suruwal* which is a churidar-like pant generally white in colour. It is worn

Sacrificing a goat to the gods and goddesses. Thousands of animals are sacrificed during 'Dasai' with official sanction.

with a black coat and a strategically shaped cap which is said to represent a Himalaya peak. The *daura or labedo* is similar to the *chowbandi choli* worn by Nepali women.

Since Nepal is an "abode of gods" the people are generally apprehensive of antagonising the gods. These gods must be kept happy and appeased. There are particular dates and months during which a certain god or goddess may be pleased with an offering. Over time some of these occasions have acquired the stature of festivals, while some of them are celebrated sombrely, each carrying with it a legend handed down the generations. They are followed by elaborate ceremonies interspersed with `tantric' rituals and offerings of animal blood, liquor and food. The sacrifices have an official sanction from the government.

Among the most popular festivals celebrated by the Nepalis is Dasai that is celebrated with gusto. It is an auspicious celebration which continues for 14 long days generally in October or November trailed by the Tihar or the festival of lights when the goddess of wealth, Lakshmi, is worshipped.

Dasai is a season of offerings made to the goddess Durga. It is also a season for expenses since every household wishes to buy goats, pigeons, or hens for sacrificial offerings to the goddess. These are later cooked at home. Elaborate dishes are prepared and children can afford to throw tantrums for new clothes on this one occasion. The elder person of the house smears a 'tika' of rice and curd in vermilion powder on the forehead reciting a long 'mantra' of blessings. It is the most enjoyable feast for children since the blessings are handed down with token money which the children eagerly wait for. Then families visit relatives carrying gifts of fruits,sweets and liquor and seeking their blessings and money. The lucky ones may get the King to apply 'tika' for them on this day who generously obliges his people who stand in long serpentine queues for this particular purpose.

During the five day celebration of *Tihar* the government allows gambling which is very popular among Nepali men. On the first day of Tihar, the crow considered to be a messenger of Yama, god of death is honoured with strings of marigold flowers and sweetmeats. The same ritual is observed with the dog the next day who, it is believed, will help them cross the river of death. Finally it is the turn of Lakshmi and the worshipping of the cow. The fourth day is the *Bhai tika* when sisters apply 'tika' made of rice paste and decorated with different types of vermilion. The brothers reciprocate by giving gifts and money. On Bhai tika begins the *deusi* which is a sort of carol singing festival of good luck and thanksgiving for the few pieces of coins that will be proferred. The head of the *deusi* wears the 'madal', a musical instrument shaped like a hollow barrel slightly large on one end and beats it melodiously, accompained by lyrics somewhat like these:—

Yasai gharko amaile/ dhunga chunda drabay houn / ai mato chunda annai houn / ai pani chunda telai houn/ ai dubo justo mauli rahun / bar-pipal jasto tapi rahun. May the mistress of this house turn stone to money / the soil to crop / water to oil / flourish like the dub grass / and grow up like the banyan and the pipal tree.

Sometimes in the city the *madal* is replaced by the blaring sound of the stereo music system accompanied by the dancing beat of the *deusi* people indicating modernity taking over traditionalism although this happens mostly in the city. But however that may be, this is the most loved occassion among the Nepalis, a time for meeting and making merry among friends and relatives.

Nepalis greet each other with joint hands saying, *namaste or namaskar.* Among the Tibetans and Sherpas, greetings or a welcoming sign is generally represented with a white scarf or *khata.* Nepalis are also perpetually in awe of the spirits that may be roaming the earth which perhaps explains some of their superstitions and beliefs. For instance, when a woman combs her hair, which she must do in the morning while sitting down, she must throw her fallen hair in a ball laced with her own spit, otherwise a wandering witch may get hold of the hair and put a curse on it which might harm the woman. Then again, one must never travel on Tuesday and return home on Saturday. Wednesday is generally considered to be a longer day, therefore travelling on this day is generally avoided. Anybody who travels on this day would take a long time to return. Similarly, one who has begun knitting a sweater on this day knows for

certain that it would take a long time to finish. Baths on *amavasya or aunshi* (pitch dark nights) are forbidden because witches are believed to bathe on these days.

Particular days of the month and year are dedicated to certain gods and goddesses. Special care is taken not to rouse the wrath of these deities. Calamities and illness, it is believed, are caused when these gods and goddesses become angry. Sometimes the very life force or spirit, it is believed, may be robbed by a supernatural entity which can be the spirit of a dead person, a witch or a demon. Toothache can be cured allegedly by hammering a nail into a block of wood in *Bangemuda* in Kathmandu; small pox can be cured by worshipping Sitala Mai, considered to be the goddess of smallpox. Promises of offering sacrifices are often made to gods and goddesses, if the ill are cured. This is done often with the help of the Shamans commonly known as *jhankris* and *dhamis*.

The *jhankri* possesses special power to invoke a certain god, goddess or a divine spirit. Once he is possessed, the divine spirit speaks through him, sometimes in a common language, at times in dialects which few may understand without the help of the Shaman's elaborate hand gestures, while he is in a trance. With the help of the divine spirit, he is able to foresee the reason for the ailing sick. He will haggle for his patient's quick recovery, pleading, ordering or requesting the spirit that holds his

Three boys all dressed up for the Gai Jatra. This festival is celebrated with humour and satire. They stage plays and theatres to mock the monarchy, the bureaucracy and the ministers.

patient's life force. He may even battle the spirit if everything fails and finally he may promise to give an egg, a hen, a pig, or some liquor perhaps in exchange for his patient's well being. Among the medicines they use are the different kinds of plants and herbs found in abundance in the kingdom.

Nepali women are fond of wearing jewelery. Married women wear *tilhari*, a gold horizontal barrel shaped ornament strewn in green or read beads known as *pote* which indicates their marital status. At times it is worn across the shoulder making the *tilhari* rest on the waist, other times it is simply worn like a necklace. Shops that sell these beads are found all over Nepal and especially near the Pashupatinath temple. Unmarried girls can wear any colour apart from red and green. The high caste Brahmin ladies and Chettris wear red sarees or blouses after marriage.

In the Kathmandu Durbar Square is the Kumari Bahal, the house of the virgin living goddess, the Kumari. This handsome house for the goddess was

Girl attendants waiting for the jhankris *at the Gosainkund.*

built by King Jaya Prakash Malla in the 18th century. Non-Hindus are not allowed inside the bahal which is an exquisite work of art in wood and like all other places in Kathmandu in particular and Nepal in general, its windows display the very fine and minute work of the Newaris. From one of these windows, the Kumari may in one of her generous moods look down upon the streets dressed in a red frock, hair tied in a knot and eyes conspicuously painted with dark kohl. She lives here accompanied by Kumarima who take care of her needs.

The Kumari can, from her window, look at the flow of tourists bargaining at the Freak Street over artifacts sold freely on the pavements right below her window. Further along the square is the place where the historical "Kot Massacre" took place that catapulted the Ranas to power, while confining the Shahs, the royal monarchs to the shadows.

Kathmandu Durbar Square is a perfect blend of history and myth, a characteristic of Nepal. Here in the heart of Kathmandu is the historical, mythical *Kasthamandap* supposed to have been carved out from a single tree. One day the tree of paradise, *Kalpabriksha*, visited a place for he wanted to see a beautiful procession passing by. He took a human form and became a spectator in the crowd until another spectator spotted him. The spectator held on to the human form of *Kalpabriksha* refusing to let him go until his demand of timber to produce a big house was met. Finally *Kalpabriksha* agreed to give the wood. From this wood was made the *Kashtamandap* , meaning the wood-home and from *Kashtamandap* was the name Kathmandu derived. Thus, Kathmandu got its name.

Festivals in Nepal are occasions of national celebration. Almost every month is a festival month, the largest one being the Dasain Tihar which every Nepali awaits eagerly. The month of Magh, which is the beginning of Nepali months,

The jhankris *dancing at the Gosainkund festival.*

begins with a ritual bath at the Narayanghat. The devouts believe that one may encounter God Shiva or Narayan himself, if the bath is undertaken in the wee hours of dawn without uttering a single word. On this day boiled vegetables, roots and fruits are eaten in solidarity to the belief that when Sita accompanied Rama to the jungle, she lived for many years on roots and fruits found in the jungle. It is followed by Basant Panchami and the Saraswati Puja. Saraswati, the goddess of learning, is worshipped by school children. Then comes the Tibetan new year Loshar and Shivratri that are celebrated on a mass scale throughout Nepal. Among the most important festivals is the Kumari Jatra. Kumari is the living goddess of Nepal. Many stories are attributed to the origin of Kumari

Following pages 64-65: *Shabru women dancing. Shabru is a Tamang village which lies to the north of Kathmandu.*

worshipping. One of them was that one day in the kingdom of King Jaya Prakash Malla, a girl developed a black eye that could destroy anybody or bring ill luck. The King banished the girl from the kingdom, fearing that evil may befall his kingdom. The girl claimed to be the incarnation of the goddess Kumari. No sooner had the King ordered the banishment, than his queen began to develop similar symptoms and possessed the spirit of the earlier Kumari. The King, alarmed at his foolishness ordered the girl to be brought back and from then on began the Kumari Jatra to appease her.

The Kumari is generally a little girl above three or four years and must be free from all blemishes. She must also possess the calmness and serenity that befits a goddess. She ceases to be a Kumari if by any chance she bleeds by getting a scratch, a cut, a falling milk tooth or when she begins her first menstrual period. Search is then on for a new Kumari which is generally during October or the month of Dasain. Her Jatra is preceded by two little boys dressed up as Ganesh and Bhairav.

Celebrated along with the Kumari Jatra is the Indra Jatra. It is a festival honouring Indra, the god of gods. The most spectacular of all Jatras, it is celebrated with mask dancing and processions. According to a legend, one day Indra was buried alive by the people of Nepal when caught stealing flowers. When his mother came pleading to the king for her son to be returned to her, an abashed king sorry for what had happened to the god, ordered a procession for Indra and his mother to be taken throughout Kathmandu. Since then Indra Jatra is observed with great gaiety. It is also the only day when the imprisoned Seto Bhairav is set free to spurt rice liquor and some live fish from his huge mouth through a pipe. Those who are lucky enough to get the live fish are assured of a good and fruitful year.

Patan Kumari just before she retires from her divinity.

In the same month of Bhadau or Bhadra is the Teej festival when women adorn their best sarees and jewelery and pray at the Pashupatinath mandir. Father's day or Gokarna Aunshi is also celebrated in this month. Similarly Mother's day which falls before the Father's day is celebrated in the month of Baisakh. On this day, mothers both living and dead are honoured. The living mothers receive gifts from children lovingly. Gai jatra is celebrated on the full moon day of August. It is a fun-filled day celebrated with humour and satire. In the olden days the monarchy was ridiculed, but these days the main targets of satire are the bureaucrats and ministers.

Nags or snakes have an auspicious and significant place in the Nepali

Facing page: An engrossed crowd under the temple.
Following pages 68-69: The Loshar (Tibetan New Year) crowd.

religion. They are feared and respected. The doors of Pashupatinath are decorated in silver with Vasuki Nag kings offering prayers to Pashupatinath. Snakes are supposed to guard the temple treasures. They are the guardians of earthquakes, rainfalls and of treasures hidden somewhere unknown.

On the fifth day of the bright lunar fortnight in the month of Shravan, the snake is worshipped. This is known as the Nag Panchami day. The doors of every household have the pictures of nagas which are glued by the bahun or pundit after the chanting of some mantra. It is held by 'gobar' or cow dung along with a few strands of `kush' grass and red vermilion.

The birthdays of Buddha, Krishna, Ganesh, the warrior-god Kumar and the King who is considered to be the incarnation of Lord Vishnu are celebrated all over the country with gusto and deep reverence. Baisakh (April and May) heralds the new year for Nepalis, and it is time to join in the Bisket Jatra. The mood is joyous at this time especially in Bhaktapur, eight miles towards the

A colourful Thimi (Thimi is a potter's village near Bhaktapur) festival crowd.

east of Kathmandu which is the venue for this celebration. Bhairav's wife Bhadrakali is the honoured guest on this day. Bedecked, she is brought out of her shrine to meet her husband in the temple of Bhairav. The celebration and worshipping goes on for four days . On the fourth and the last day, a pole with a lingam on top and banners on either side signifying two evil snakes, male and female (that once lived inside the nose of a princess) is brought down. It signifies the death of evil and the passing of that year. Henceforth the people of Nepal look towards happier times with the commencing new year.

A whole year passes bringing in again the same festivals, colours, fun and gaiety, prayers and offerings of flowers, sweets and vermilion and sacrifices of animals for the extremely religious people of this country, drenched deeply in their own exotic culture.

Facing page: *A Lama masked dance in Boudha.*

71

Flora and Fauna

———— ✱ ————

$\mathcal{N}$epal is home to a fascinating variety of wild flowers, animals and butterflies. In the peaceful solitude of the countryside, in and around Kathmandu valley, one finds the red rhododendron, whose colour changes from light yellow, light pink and purple to white. The *laligurans* (*lali*, red; *gurans*, rhododendron) was made the national flower of Nepal in 1962. *Gurans* evoke fond and nostalgic memories of the home, the hills and the mountains. A Nepali woman's blushing red cheeks are always described as *laligurans*. More than 30 different varieties of rhododendrons can be found, from two inches high to more than 30 feet tall. Some species emit

Left: *An exotic variety of the rich and fascinating repertoire of wild flowers found in Nepal.*
Right: *A wild flower blooming in peaceful solitude in the high altitudes.*

a strong smell that can make one unconscious. The less dangerous ones are used extensively for decorations or as offerings to gods. Shamans use them elaborately during certain rituals, and a few particular species are used as burning twigs or incense. Certain types of rhododendrons can also be brewed into wine. The famous sal (*Shorea robusta*) tree whose leaves are used for making plates (*tapari*), is found in the Terai and lower Siwalik regions of Nepal. The sal has a kind of creeper that grows clockwise around it. According to a myth, if you ever happen to see the creeper growing anti-clockwise, all you need to do is hammer a nail into it and the tree will turn into gold overnight! Nepal's forests have an abundance of ferns and herbs which have been used for therapeutic purposes from times immemorial. Modern medicine has also discovered their value for the treatment of stomach or respiratory ailments.

The stinging nettle (*Girardinia*) or Sisnu whose tender offshoots, cooked together with rice, are relished by the villagers is also found extensively in the forests. It is said that a Tibetan yogi by the name of Minaku survived for fourteen years on this plant alone. The paper used in making envelopes and calendars in Nepal is produced from the Damphe shrub, whose importance is second only to *laligurans*. Almost every shop in Nepal is named after it.

Any mention of the flora of Nepal would be incomplete without the mention of the beautiful orchids which grow in abundance in the hills. There are 319 species of this flower in Nepal. Among plants with well known medicinal properties is the lichen which is also used as a spice and incense. Its extract is used to make perfume.

Left: A species of the beautiful and rare orchid grown in abundance in the hills.
***Right:** Laligurans (lali-red, gurans-rhododendron)— the national flower of Nepal— can be spotted towards the midhills in and around Kathmandu valley.*

The Terai is full of animals like the elephants, gaur, rhinoceros, leopard, tiger and the wild goat. The best time to see wildlife in the jungles of Nepal is from February to June but usually October to June is also good for going on a safari. Extensive poaching had led to the extinction of the rhino which was hunted for its horns, but wildlife reserves were established to put a stop to this. Other wildlife include the musk deer, the blue sheep the snow leopard and the yak. The 614 species of butterflies include the swallowtails. Nepal is also a paradise for bird-watchers as it has 400 species of birds. The blood pheasant, golden-breasted tit-babbler, shrike babbler and the brown parrotbill can easily be spotted as also the accentors, redstarts, golden eagle and the Himalayan griffon vulture.

Chapter 4
— ❋ —
Peaks and Trekkings

*I*n an early winter dawn when the meagre rays of the elusive sun reach down to touch the dew-laden trees, they must first go past the Himalayas brushing across the glorious triangular peaks until they glow with a golden colour, finally resting on the dome of Swayambhunath and then gradually spreading towards the temples across the valley. To a visiting foreigner the awesome majestic Himalaya is a thing of beauty, to behold, praise, touch and scale to unfurl the secrets that lie behind these mountains. To a native it is the holiest of holy places where the gods dwell, where sounds of tinkling bells are heard with the wind and where an attempt to unravel the mysteries might invoke the wrath of the gods. Therefore they had to be preserved, the gods appeased with incense, prayer flags and flowers offered and hymns sung in praise of them. Yet the peaks have been scaled time and again, their magnetic attraction defying the very rationality of mankind.

Nepal decided to bare the mysteries of the mountains during the 1950's. Since then the commercial prospects of mountaineering and trekking have been growing at a phenomenal rate in Kathmandu, providing employment to many. Although almost fifty percent visitors to Kathmandu are Indians who come in the hope of doing business, or fulfilling religious sentiments, the other half are mainly foreigners who come for mountaineering and trekking, ready to face the rigorous hardships and probably the loss of lives incurred during these expeditions. Initially, the expeditions were scientific in nature. Much before the opening of the mountains, the first European to discover the charms of mountain magnificence from afar was James Renell who was a geographer and a map maker. His discovery that some of the mountains were as high as 8000 meters in 1788 left many gasping with disbelief, but provided them with a strong urge to find the truth. He was followed by Sir George Everest, Surveyor-General of India who also gave his consent to lend his name to the mountain.

Even when history began changing in this mountainous valley with British residents stationed in Kathmandu, expeditions were never allowed until 1949. The opportunity of scaling these mountains with the awesome thought of actually being able to put their foot deep into the snow brought many spirited foreigners to Nepal, especially those who had had the good luck of scaling the alpine pleasures of European mountains, but had been restricted to these alone.

Among the most coveted one was Mount Everest, the highest at 8,848 meters and known as Sagarmatha in Nepali. The Tibetans called it Chomolungma, or the Mother Goddess. For decades this beautiful mountain lured great mountaineers from all over the world without success until finally just two days after the first summit bid by Charles Evans and Tom Bourdillon, Edmund Hilllary along with the man who made the Sherpas' name rise in glory in the history of mountaineering, Tenzing Norgay Sherpa stood on the summit proudly on the fine day of 29th May, 1953. Thereafter among those who successfully completed the assault on this peak are Reinhold Messner, an Italian who was

Facing page: *A 'chorten' and a prayer flag in Tangbuche.*

Mount Everest.

Mount Makalu.

Mount Machapuchare (Fish Tail).

Mount Choyu.

Mount Thumserku.

Mount Kanchenjunga.

Mount Langtang (Peace Mountain).

Mount Amadablam.

the first to climb it without the use of oxygen and alone (without the help of the Sherpas), Ang Phu Sherpa of Nepal who scaled it from two different routes, Mrs Junko Tabei of Japan-the first woman to climb the Everest and Ang Rita Sherpa who scaled it ten times. The American, Dick Bass, was the oldest to scale it at the age of fifty plus and more recently, the latest to achieve the feat was Tenzing Norgay Sherpa's son.

The Himalayas boast of the eight highest mountains in the world. Of these, the Kanchenjunga, 8,586 meters (28,169 ft.), known for its beauty and numerous peaks—four of which are more than 8,000 meters—go on to the adjacent neighbourhood of Darjeeling and Sikkim while the Everest (29,028 feet) touches Tibet. The Kanchenjunga is by far the most well documented mountain. This mountain range which is the landmark of Darjeeling and Sikkim is featured in many folk lores and folk songs of the Nepalis. Many a time the Nepali belle is compared to the beauty of Kanchenjunga and immortalised in poetry. It is so

Member of the Nepal Mountaineering Association. Standing second from the right is Ang Rita Sherpa, a world record holder having scaled the Everest ten times.

sacred that four climbers who reached its summit were forbidden to tread on it by the Sikkimese Government, lest its purity be defiled, inviting the wrath of the gods.

The fourth highest peak Lhotse, 8516 meters (27,940 ft.) was climbed solo by a Yugoslavian sports journalist without oxygen in 1990. The southern part of the Lhotse was described as the most difficult passage by the well-known climber, Reinhold Messner. Makalu, 8,463 meters (27,766 ft.) was scaled by the French along with Americans and New Zealanders. Cho Oyu or the Turquoise Goddess, 8,201 meters (26,906 ft.) was scaled by Dr. Herbert Tichy, a Viennese who experienced the feeling of paradise with frostbitten fingers that occurred

Following pages 78-79: *Tangboche monastery. Once destroyed by fire, it has now been restored.*

during the ascent. Similarly,the ascent of Dhaulagiri meaning pure white mountain at 8,167 meters (26, 795 ft.) was completed when a team of Europeans with two Sherpas set foot on the summit in 1960. It was the last peak to be climbed as earlier attempts to scale this mountain had been unsuccessful. Manaslu 8,163 meters (26,781 ft.) was scaled by the Japanese, Nepalis and South Koreans thus making it quite an Asian territory.

The first among these peaks to be scaled was the Annapurna, 8,091 meters (26,545 ft.). The scaling success of this peak opened the opportunities for other mountaineers to attempt the remaining seven peaks. The first to make the attempt was a strong French expedition team which did face difficulties, but its success was a landmark in mountaineering history. The altitude problems are many. At a higher level it becomes difficult for the body to adjust; the thinking process becomes slow and several visions may dominate the mind. Climbers at times loose body fluid at high altitudes resulting in dehydration. Spells of

Gokyo lake. One can have a close beautiful view of the Everest from Gokyo.

unconsciousness are known difficulties faced by unacclimatised mountaineers. Thus, when Messner claimed to have climbed the Everest without the help of oxygen, eyebrows were raised in disbelief, but he proved them wrong when he did it again. Since then many have done it yet again and established the fact that the Himalayas can indeed be scaled without any aid, but only the fittest with a strong will power and faith in good luck can attempt it.

Mountaineering has given people in Nepal, especially the Sherpas a new lease of economic life. Dreams of being educated and speaking English with foreigners have taken over. The great mountaineer Hillary himself was responsible for introducing education to most Sherpa children with the establishment of the Himalayan Trust. Alongside, trekking too has developed enormously. It has become the most important means for raking in foreign exchange for the Nepalese exchequer.

The picturesque valley of Nepal is a trekker's paradise. The object of the trekkers is that of travelling by foot while observing the surrounding beauty and famous cultural or historical sites. Besides its potential for adventure, it is also regarded as a fine way of testing one's fitness. The grim trail of the arduous mountains spotted with smiling natives, the rarest of orchids and varieties of rhododendrons that spread out colourfully on the slopes makes trekking a lifetime experience. The wrong notion of trekking however, is that all one requires is the ability to walk. This may be right as far as trekking the countryside is concerned, but trekking the peaks requires a minimum knowledge of using ropes and ice axes.

The trekking peaks, usually at the foothills of the mountains, ranging from a height of 5,587 meters (18,330 ft.) to 6,654 meters (21,830 ft.) are declared free to be scaled at a reasonable trekking fee. But a Sherpa guide is a must. There are 18 such peaks identified, the most popular ones being the Khumbu and the

Manang with the turquoise lake and Annapurna range. Manang lies on the trekking route of the Annapurna circuit.

Annapurna Himal. The trekking peaks are a stepping stone to scaling the bigger mountains like the Everest. Among the trekking peaks, the known ones are Mera Peak, 6,654 meters (21,831 ft.), Chulu East or Gundang 6,584 meters (21,601 ft.), Fluted peak or Singu Chuli 6,501 meters (21,329 ft.), Hiumchuli or literally translated as Snow Peak, 6,441 meters, (21,132 ft.), Chulu West 6,419 meters (21,560 ft.), Kusum Kanguru, 6,367 meters (20,889 ft.), Parchamo 6,187 meters (20,298 ft.), Imja Tse, 6,160 meters (20,210 ft.), Lobuche East Peak, 6,119 meters (20,075 ft.), Pisang Peak 6,091 meters (19,983 ft.), Kwangde, 6,011 meters (19,721 ft.), Paldor 5,896 meters (19,344 ft.), Kongma tse, 5,849 meters (19,190 ft.), Naya Kanga or Ganja la Chuli, 5,844 meters (19,180 ft.), Pokalde (Dolma Ri) 5,806 meters (19,049 ft.), Tent Peak 5,663 meters (18,580 ft.), Ramdung 5,925 meters (19,435 ft.), and Mardi Himal 5,587 meters (18,330 ft.). These 18 peaks are the best for vacation trekking and are also considered to be hasslefree as

far as the Nepal bureaucracy is concerned, for the larger mountain expeditions must have permission from the higher authorities.

Two hundred kilometers to the west of Kathmandu is the famous Pokhra, a celebrated place for Indian and native honeymooners who like to roam the banks of the Phewa lake located here. Nestled directly below the Annapurna range of mountains, Pokhra is the favourite haunt of travellers, for Annapurna directly across in view is the most popular of all trekking peaks. October to May is considered to be the trekking season, although many seasoned trekkers opt for winter too. Royal Nepal Airlines flies directly to Pokhra twice a day and is only 35 minutes away from Kathmandu.

Pokhra is the ideal place for beginning a trekking expedition. The most enchanting thing about Pokhra is the magnificent view of the Machapuchere, or the Fish Tail Peak that is reflected on a clear sunny day in the waters of the Phewa lake.

A wooden suspension bridge near Namche bazaar.

Annapurna I is just 30 miles across from the lake and almost 40,000 trekkers visit the mountain every year, their route mostly crossing the Annapurna mountains numbered as Annapurna I, II, III, and IV and Gangapurna. On the northern side of the Annapurna is the Manang, popular with the trekkers too. More than 200 trekkers pass through the Manang during the peak trekking season. The Manang Mountaineering School built in 1979 offers a course on climbing techniques. While descending one comes across the second holiest place apart from Pashupatinath of Nepal, the Muktinath. It is sacred to both Hindus and Buddhists and is considered to be the holiest pilgrimage.

The trek normally begins from Dumre which is about a four hours drive from Pokhra. It then continues through Magar, Thakali, and interesting Gurung

Facing page: *People being pulled across on a ropeway manually.*

villages in their unadulterated purity. The surrounding mountains, as if bursting from the earth itself to reach the skyline look down silently to the trekker's delight. One can see the Manaslu 8,163 meters (27,781 ft.), Himalchuli 7,893 meters (25,896 ft.), Nagdi Himal 7,835 meters (25,705 ft.) and Baudha Himal 6,672 meters (21,889 ft.) so near that an urge to touch it may overcome you. The most risky and treacherous pass on the way is the Namun Bhanjang pass which is 5,502 meters (18,050 ft.).

Among the trekkers another famous destination is the Langtang valley at an altitude of almost 10,000 feet. The Langtang peak is 32,771 feet. The Langtang people are generally of Tibetan origin and live on a diet of roasted potatoes. They also grow buckwheat and barley. This trekking paradise is well known for its glacial beauty, the simple people that spot the hills and stunning mountains. The route generally proceeds along Langtang-Gosainkund-Helambu and is considered to be one of the difficult treks. Yaks can be seen on these trails.

Stupa outside the Lo Manthang gate (Mustang). Mustang, a Tibetan kingdom with its own king (now a subject of the Nepal monarchy) is located to the far north of Nepal and was closed to foreigners till very recently.

Trekkers can drive upto Trisuli and then to Dhunche which is the entrance point for Langtang National Park. A wide variety of rhododendron blooms here and rich wild life including musk deer, leopard and langur monkeys can be spotted if one is lucky.

The Gosainkund lake at 4,328 meters (14,200 ft.) is a religious pilgrimage site for thousands of devotees of Shiva. Hindus take a bath in the holy waters to renew their devotion to Shiva. It is believed that Shiva threw his trishul which stuck in the mountain out of which gushed three springs. Gosainkund is one of them. Thousands of shamans come here to bathe and renew their faith in Shiva on a particular day, singing and dancing in a trance around the lake. According to a legend, one day a ghole *jhankri,* a shaman of a particular class wanted to kill a serpent who lived in the lake. By killing the serpent he would have become materially prosperous and could have acquired whatever he wished for.

Accompanied by his wife and the drum that shamans beat while dancing to its tune, he reached the banks of the lake. He ordered his wife to beat the drum while keeping her eyes tightly shut and warned her that on no account should she open her eyes, while he did the rest, slipping into a trance. For a long time the wife beat the drum but on hearing strange noises couldn't restrain herself from opening her eyes. Her first sight was that of her husband in the lake battling a ferocious *nag*-a serpent. Terror struck her and she fled the scene. The shaman was never seen thenceforth. From that day onwards the ghole *jhankris* vowed never to take their wives to the lake. Climbing from the Gosainkund lake, one can reach the Sing gompa. Located here is a cheese factory that churns out cheese made of Yak milk.

A little higher along the east side of the lake is the Helambu. Helambu is inhabited by Sherpas. Many of the Sherpas run rest houses and serve tea. They are kept very neat and tidy. The Paanch Pokhari is located in Helambu . The

Namche Bazaar with Jhorima in the back. Namche is the main village on the route to Everest.

return route from Helambu can be from Chautara, a market or through the lake Bhairav kund splattered with Sherpa and Tamang villages. Balephi ends the trek and then it is back to Kathmandu by road.

Trekkers trekking in west Nepal must be extra cautious of their eatables and should carry the required amount for the days to be trekked, as no tea houses can be seen here. The area is dominated by Thakuris, a high caste but a rung below Brahmins, who will not tolerate the defiling of their house by allowing strangers, especially foreigners inside their house, which also invites wrath from their closed society.

Trekking in Nepal is a well organised industry. Many may think a trekking entourage comprising of cooks, porters and the head sherpa known as the

Following pages 86-87: *Mount Annapurna 1 and Fang at sunrise.*

85

sardar, a bit too much for a trekking team of two or three, but it is often worth it and nobody complains. The cooks are trained to swiftly dish up western, continental and Chinese food, if the regular Nepali meal of dal and bhat (rice) with a dash of green vegetables is found to be too monotonous. It is always better to plan a trekking holiday through experts available at the experienced trekking organisations, the best one being Mountain Travels owned by Lt. Col. James Roberts.

As an officer in the British Indian Army, Roberts had earlier had the opportunity of climbing several peaks in Nepal. Today, many of the Sherpas own their own trekking organisations, such as the Sherpa Trekking Service: Sherpa Society. The other well known one is the Annapurna Trekking and Mountaineering Pvt. Ltd. Almost all of them provide excellent camping equipments, food cooked on kerosene stoves and generally an English speaking

Sherpa ladies at Tangboche wait for the arrival of Sir Edmund Hillary.

sardar. The porters, mainly Sherpas, toil with the heaviest of luggage through the trekking path without any complaint. Most of them find it a profitable enterprise. The advantage of going on a trekking expedition with a well known agency is that it provides all the necessary facilities, right from obtaining the required permission, to good porters to transportation and equipments. They also guide one to penetrate the deepest of the Himalayan wilderness through a maze of rich wild life, flora and fauna.

Apart from providing the physical fitness challenge, a trek often offers a chance to go through a personal introspection. The fresh air of the mountains, the mysticism, encounters with tribes who practise the pre-Buddhist Bon religion,

Facing page: *"Namaste" greetings from the Sherpa land.*
Following pages 90-91: *Cattles returning home at sunset.*

the innocence of the villagers dotting the high altitude mountains, the stone gompas, the sacred lakes, the mere wind loaded with the spirituality of years of worshipping and chanting is enough to invoke questions that haunt mankind. Indeed, one may return as a completely changed person from the trip.

The past few years have seen a number of speciality trekking packages added to a trip. According to one's liking, the trekking can double up as a cultural study of the inhabitants who live high up in the montains. Indeed their primitive lifestyle, clothes and food have been a subject of study for many people who are interested in the sociological patterns of a clan or a tribe. Besides, trained instructors can guide one through a course of yoga or meditation in the fresh air of the mountains. Other activities like sketching in the wild and birdwatching can also be made a part of vacation trekking. Just as the Himalayas are sacred to Nepalis, so are the various rivers that flow through Nepal, for water is the source of life. Moreover, Hindus believe that

Rafting in the Trishuli river. Rafting is one of the most popular river sports in Nepal.

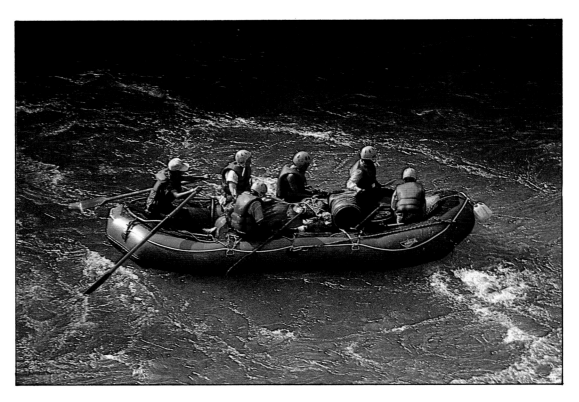

the ashes of the dead, if merged in the holy waters, open the gateway to reach the heavens. Additionally, rivers in Nepal provide various adventures to tourists interested in water sports, especially the white water river rafting and kayaking.

Many come for the combined excitement of trekking and river-rafting in the country while many come specifically for river-rafting. One of the five rivers that are permitted for river-rafting are the Seti nadi, or the white river. Rafters can hardly contain their joy at the virgin white water gushing and streaming ferociously down from Pokhra to Chitwan. Nepali rafters are experts and trained guides in safety procedures. Away from the city, the experience of going through these waters along with the white torrents, across the beautiful rural countryside with enchanting views can be a memorable one.

While on the subject of rivers, the experience of fishing Mahseer that thrive in the cold waters of the Kosi and Karnali rivers can be fascinating. Fishes like Katli and Asla make for good catches, to be roasted while trekking. Last but not the least is the experimentation with new adventures like mountain biking, paragliding and ballooning, which are yet to pick up in these mountains.

While adventure sports bring the much needed foreign exchange to boost the economy of Nepal, the negative aspect has been the obvious onslaught on the Himalayas. The Himalayas littered with empty cans and toilet papers are not only hurting the Nepali sentiments but the environment as well. The strong lobby of environmentalists in Nepal is fully aware of the consequences, urging the guides to keep the Himalayas clean. Most of the guides are trained to protect the environment, by laying down rules of sanitation during these trails, and trekkers are advised to follow them keeping in mind the sanctity of the mountains, rivers and the environment.

A village near Baglung (west Nepal) with mustard blooming on the terraces.

Nepal Today

Nepal's capital Kathmandu is a very congested city, where pollution is very high, with a population increasing day by day. This is apparent if one wanders through the narrow by-lanes of Kathmandu, elbow to elbow with bleeting cows, honking Toyotas, cycle rickshaws and tourists. It is no wonder that more and more Nepalis of the valley are resorting to moving towards the Terai and taking to farming, unmindful of the tropical heat. The Terai or the tropical zone of Nepal is responsible for growing much of the rice that the country is so fond of. During the season lush green beds of rice, swaying to the gentle beat of the wind, convey a gentle greeting. It may be days before one hears the rhythmical sound of thrashing of the crop to the ground by ladies clad in ankle-length sarees that make work easier, aided by the strong hands of their menfolk.

In the earlier days, the Terai—a place of hot winds—represented fear in the form of malaria. Today the Terai however, is growing rapidly in terms of industrial development. Biratnagar which is the second largest city in Nepal, was the first to establish Nepal's very first industry in 1936, the Biratnagar Jute Mills. Because of its geographical position more mills like the sugar and textile mills and industries in kitchenware have come up following the Second World War. Roads are now being built across the Terai and most of the jungles here are fast disappearing and taking their place are houses, long roads for transportation and busy bazaars. Four decades ago, visitors to Kathmandu either travelled by foot or on horseback. Today there are modern roads and a railway line from the Indian border running upto Janakpur.

Kathmandu is increasingly becoming aware of the pressing demands of globalisation and gearing up to face the challenges of a modern world. The onslaught of satellite communication has crossed the threshold of Nepali homes,

Mount Fishtail and Annapurna and Phewa Taal (Pokhra) in the early morning. Pokhra is a popular destination for trekkers and tourists.

making a tremendous impact on their lifestyle today. Star TV, MTV and Channel V have gripped the hearts of young Nepalis, the impact of which is seen in the dressing and eating habits. Fast food, along with traditional Tibetan food like momos, thukpas and Nepali dishes like rice and dal are fast making inroads. For those whose palates do not agree with the native dishes, choices ranging from Indian, Italian, Chinese to Continental dishes can be available readily. The all time favourite haunt for most westerners in Nepal is Freak Street in the Kathmandu Durbar Square, widely associated with the hippies in the 1960's, which now sells various knick-knacks like curio items and art objects, and Thamel where a large variety of small restaurants and bars remain open till midnight.

The plethora of hotels in Nepal provide assurance of a comfortable stay, vying with each other to provide optimum satisfaction to the visitor. There are four five-star hotels that include Soaltee, Oberoi, Yak and Yeti, Annapurna and Everest; seven four star, five three star, three two star and six one star hotels, apart from many small guest houses and lodges to suit budget travellers. In Pokhra, the second favoured destination after Kathmandu, plans are already afoot to make a base for aerial adventure sports like gliding, hand gliding, ballooning and according to latest reports, the possible installation of a cable car system. New hotels like the Dusit Thani Phulbari, the Bangkok-based hotel chain boasting all modern facilities like the sauna, health centre, mini golf course are all set to change the face of tourism in Pokhra. With the majority of the 19 million population depending on agriculture and farming for a livelihood, Nepal has to depend heavily on foreign aid for its economic development. It is classified by the United Nations as one of the world's least developed nations, with a very low per capita income, even when compared to other developing nations. The rate of literacy is very low with poor health care

Mani stones on the trekking route (Buddhist prayers).

facilities. Moreover, with a population growth of almost 3 per cent, it has to depend heavily on its Indian neighbour for trade and daily necessities.

However, on the whole, Nepal has withstood the onslaught of Western culture, while imbibing only its best advantageous aspects. Much of the rural charm has been retained despite the fact that ethnic villages have been penetrated by the outside world, mainly trekkers, hikers and mountain bikers carrying in their rucksacks a variety of modern goodies. In fact, adventure-seeking tourists are forewarned about the sensitivities and superstitions of these ethnic people dwelling high in the villages. Thus, Nepal has so far retained the mystery, rustic charm and beauty that it offers every passing day to foreigners who throng its lanes, by-lanes, hotels, restaurants and mountains in thousands.

Following page 96: *Children looking through the typically Nepali carved windows.*